OUR CHROME ARMS OF GYMNASIUM

OUR CHROME ARMS OF GYMNASIUM

Poems by Crystal Curry

*Winner of the 2009
Slope Editions Book Prize*

slopeeditions

NEW HAMPSHIRE NEW YORK MASSACHUSETTS

©2010 Crystal Curry
Published by Slope Editions

Graphic design by Adam Grano

Library of Congress Cataloging-in-Publication Data

Curry, Crystal, 1974–
  Our chrome arms of gymnasium : poems / by Crystal Curry.
    p. cm.
  ISBN 978-0-9777698-5-8 (alk. paper)
  I. Title.
  PS3603.U7749O97 2010
  811'.6--dc22
                        2010032516

FOR COR

CRYSTAL CURRY CAN'T STOP FOOLING AROUND WITH WORDS

by Dara Wier

There she goes … uninhibited with alliterative, syncopated many-beated word conglomerations. She writes like a glacier on speed, like a glacier unknowing of its boundaries, like a glacier singing and saying its way through histories private to it and public to us. These poems leave behind not little but huge traces of heart and mind, fueled—because gravity is a kind of fuel—with forces of nature and fissures through which to see and know a little better humanity's funny, frangible place in it all.

Sometimes the combined force of words seems furious and angry and exasperated and charged up with emotional syllables beyond plain ole common sense; other times a line will register a note of woe so forlorn one wants to offer one's services as its professional mourner.

Sometimes she is out-tender-buttoning Tender Buttons because this book doesn't have that riddling next-step-is-yours mindset, it has already gone the distance logical and rational steps usually go and goes far, far out there where only poetry goes.

Don't get me wrong, I love Miss Stein and all her fervent writing ways, it's just that she was writing in a different age and for another time, bless her soul. She was not poetry hot, she was reason driven, she was math accurate and less spirit immaculate and more mature than any of us will ever be. She was a natural big baby, an eternally old one, and I love her, too.

Crystal Curry is another kind. She has the fury of a new young movie that is never-endingly gripping; that movie's soundtrack is the best one ever; that soundtrack beats everything else in its tracks and it acts for us as few stories ever can.

Don't get me wrong, I'm crazy about a good story. Ms. Curry hints that she's known a lot of stories in her time. She hints and she feints when her gambit provokes. She's some kind of trigger, she says so somewhere. She says somewhere she knows something about "Our pomp pop pop …" and it how it slaps "in concert with the heartstock manifesto machine."

TABLE OF CONTENTS

Introduction   6.
Preface   10.

I.
Eileen   19.
Delta   21.
Executive Branch   22.
Automated Floorness/Ceilingness
    Questionnaire   23.
Floyd & Tad, in Tandem   25.
Brigadier Rory Gentle   26.
The Recidivists   27.
That Which We Pull From Air Has
    Always Been   28.
The Vernaculous Off-Journey Of   29.
Papa November   30.

II.
Love Chant   33.
Cherries   36.
I Wouldn't Call it 'Je Ne Sais Quoi,'
    Exactly   37.
The Corporeal Other   39.
How I Explain Myself to Former,
    Current & Potential Husbands   40.
Drink To   41.
Sky-Lit Hi   47.
Tragedy   48.

III.
Decree   51.
Teaser   52.
Personal   53.
Notice   54.

Rite   55.
Toast   56.
Warning   57.
Vow   58.
Confession   59.
Warranty   60.
Moral   61.
Tract   62.

IV.
Ontography   65.
A Succession of Blackshirts   69.
Trinity w/Citrus   70.
Barn   72.
My One Paneled Wall   74.
Hand, Floor, Galaxy   75.
Small Things Industries   77.
Cha-Cha-Cha   78.

V.
Tu Quoque   83.
To Not Be Perplexed
    About the Givens   84.
The Flowers of Kungshallen   85.
Sitting The Batologist   87.
Alphabug   89.
Virtue, Continence,
    Incontinence, Vice   91.
The Star Children   93.
The Fallacy of Misleading
    Vividness   94.

Acknowledgements   96.

PREFACE
by Crystal Curry

Last run in the roseberries: relinquished past. The gunless plain is silent, save this wind. You are a plague, a harbinger of three swell-worn ships. I wear a bracelet of constellations—nothing more. What lies beneath the valleys and hills has already already been: a scrawling of a vial, on a wall, a scratching of spermatozoa in the grit. My open hand cuts through the air in a path already made. Tongue of land, a triune to tune my eye. A starchart, I hold to your hip. A promise of hereafter, here before we bartered it. And with one touch, you leak the righteous horizon and holy albumen. You put gold between my teeth, and it is always genuine.

Burgeoning, afresh, in the synergetic mote. The consequents rise and pitch, in the semi-square. You are always just about to become. I wear a charged possibility— nothing more. What energy we gather is ours to append. The sympathetic atoms are hysterical, flush. My buttons and hadrons are always and all but undone. A dream in which we're drawn to run our hands over the same cold rails, again. The delineation starts with a pulse of suggestion. An appeal to join, to split, and to, ultimately, re-join. In yesterday's coil, it all means y to me, now. It is even less total, the second, seventh, billionth time around.

Whizzing, the object of the gaze. The bleachers are full, and rowdy. You are the hairs on the back of the neck. I am wearing a cloud of dust—nothing more. What we will do is thirty laps. A mad exhibition, in mid-afternoon. My pistons and pinwheels are fixed and primed, at the start. The happening they expect is a heart in the throat. Butterfly belly, a high unquotidian. A readying, here in the heat of so many eyes—with the crunching and anthems and rote people noise. Everything every bit as death-defying as it seems to seem. The motordrome opens its "O," for the season.

When the red parade ends, the meat locker is quiet. The petty bodies of the last miraculous harvest, hung. You are a long-term picture. I wear the praxes of agriculture—nothing more. What telling there is is always good: the ever-smiling faithful in the *Tournedos News*. But, my heart holds out for a mobilization frenzy. Outside, birds perch on the waste bins, awash in the gross milk and the gross honey. With each step forward, we are a millenarian transformation: a beak, pushing its point into the bloody membranes. "*This is revolution,*" you say, I say, "*This is doom,*" and Lenin sinks his bronze roots amongst the mums—

EILEEN

Janet is fucking
my public defender. They've been together
for fourteen weeks. They are both
disestablishmentarians: the budding spring
of love download.

Janet is the one
for my garbage collector. Janet is the daughter
of Dr. Pocket. Janet sometimes wears
a white blouse with red flowers. Janet
is very, very sexy, for a Pocket.

It is necessary
to keep order in a prison. My crying
is due to sudden boredom or illness. Janet
& my therapist are totally doing it: the plebeian ecstasy
of love Christmas.

Janet is known as
the queen of cockalorum. I am
the leader of the popinjays. Janet is sleeping
with my dead father, who is still very slim
& catches cars in his tendrils.

All the ladies
have their blue laws & curse. All the gentlemen
have their wither & taxonomy. Janet is knocking boots
with my astrologer: the costermonger
of love autopsy.

Janet is sitting
on my jungle-print couch. Janet is waiting

for my telephone installer. I am the president
of Buddha Gaya. Janet is eating
a cinnamon cruller.

DELTA

Phenom: un-usually hurried agape
to my bacon & squadron
I am a delicate
born in a war widow's lacy black
a real good lay in a fallout
armpit
keeps the cigarettes
from getting wet
a torture a red ribbon barrow on flag day
we storm the parade & kill
all three
out of four un-dressed aggressors
agree:

she's a dirty pig   let her in

                   & a porkbelly

stuffs
everyone silly
on furlough for paterfamilias stand
in deed
& declaration of a white-
hot blast the frazzle-
gutted churlish

         charley...   my love sling

EXECUTIVE BRANCH

With due respect to Article II of the U.S. Constitution

Women
at desks: de-smocked & Marzipan
Girl's a surrogate: cordial
cloud. Daddy:
digest
a zero-defendant. *As he*
shall think proper, he
shall receive.

Grain bearers: frisk & fallow. Marzipan
Cloud: my bushels
closed
to this. Daddy This: *which*
shall
expire. Women
at desks, bound with
licorice: yes.

Grain bearers: *by & with*
the consent. Daddy Consent: a move
to strike. Women
at desks: s'all
sarcoid & auricle. Mar-
zipan Zero: a spurious
peck.

The grain bearers' thrust:
a little
shoot. Marzipan Pecked: the berry
of me. Women
at desks: delicious. Daddy
Digest:
the power
to fill up all vacancies.

AUTOMATED FLOORNESS/ CEILINGNESS QUESTIONNAIRE

Do

you sweat

the petrogarchs? Do you wash

in order, then? Is

your blood

robustly good? Does it earn

which forfeiture? Is

the outcome

fairly pall? When you

sweep

does it make a broom? Conniption

of a butterfly? Shrill note

across expanse of room? Do they

hold your inklings

nigh? Are you a clue? Is this

because? Is stuff you engender

immune

to the freeze? *Are you less*

a cunt

*then you were last yea*r? Are you

standing

in the way? Till the windfall comes? Till

Mother's day? And mother? Did she

like to whistle? Did she

whistle

in the yard? Until the shavers

chased her in? You did him

in an alleyway? Suffered, wrongly? Smoke

or honey? Will you

drink

the potion, love? Do you love
the symphony? Are you
sympathetic,
still?

FLOYD & TAD, IN TANDEM

Here I come over the poppy-covered hill, you put your gray cap on.

I etched you a rose in glass, carved "Tad" in my headboard, sanded it down.

I'll play like it's late in the war, & the outposts have fell, I promise good.

I grab my knees, solstice, equinox, pre-op, post-op, wash, rinse, spin.

I'll bring over my little bag of beans, tin cup & cast-iron pot.

When one actor bows low, the other actor can put his boot on him.

Floyd, we are tangled up, parts touching we didn't know we had or did that.

Tad, we're tangled up & they're coming up our dirt path a-stomping.

Floyd, even as you go down, the Dow goes up & up, I sometimes follow it.

Tad, what musket & ash tree—did you wrap that train track around it.

Floyd, I say you come to the kiosk every sixth Thursday, bring monte casino.

Floyd, our Tad is a good man, turns his cups upside down to dry, smart & efficient.

Tad, Floyd is good with numbers, likes tapestries & the Battle Hymn of the Republic.

BRIGADIER RORY GENTLE

But, I was a trigger, a death throe cramped, kenophobic, in your variegated helmet.

A sovereign entity, hilltop vidette, the eyes & ears of this essential important.

I can slide up on a stool, slip up & say: *I'm a private privates private.*

I'll know you, then forget you, remember a crumpled one-time of sweet code later.

You showcase that musculature, radical & nonpareil, candily headlamp & lewd.

We're a fit fit fit & what you'll think you see is my centurion slide out, is my shoe.

Grapple with the order, hoary morality, shoot up the ballroom, shake down the latrine.

I'll cinch my shorts, Fort Trocadero, bar the door, tuck in safe, the rusting heirlooms.

Our pomp pop pop & slap in concert with the heartstock manifesto machine.

All juiced, my juicy, your scoping me & I am a flat nutrient beneath the wheel.

We're an articulated movement, fell & felt a notion in the cover of wheatgrass, again.

THE RECIDIVISTS

Thou be'st a creature, faux, electrified, partially a-skitter, by the rule of law.

I'll be'st commandment, hill of gravel, what I sayeth out loud is so damning, anymore.

Imprisonment will do thou well, shiny claws, straight antennae, no trouble everyplace.

What I sayeth is ye be a body present, findeth clean hooves that will groweth green.

We'll liveth in an outcrop, bumpeth our shells together, carrot & parsnip, until.

I'll batheth in blood be'st Queen Quality World, a walk, all-clean & all-consumable.

Ye, saved, shall gorgeth on high, thou dost always habeas corpus in the dark.

Ye chooseth to behaveth, bringeth cherries in bed, but once a defiler, always a defiler.

I'll be'st ok, from guts to rennet, more permissible, but knoweth my tree is only three.

Ye turneth it around, maketh it happen on the inside, food turneth fast to flesh unto me.

Thou mayeth haveth it, maketh it part of thee & I'll playeth a mouthful of hoopoe.

Be ye holy, for I am holy & I shall putteth none of the crushed bones unto thee.

THAT WHICH WE PULL
FROM AIR HAS ALWAYS BEEN
—After Thomas Howard

C flat
is dead & gone. She never was. She
was never culled. No borzoi
ever could
outlast a mendicant
in bed—was that the will
of God? We guess.

An alien raps
his alien head—

when will they fix that hole for good?

Then,
he watches Kay & Capital Rex
negotiate another go,
another template, snatched
& kept
that snatch
real wet. For them. For us.
For a cock-loving lens &
a lens-loving cock. "*Slow down,*"
she says & then, we cut
to a similar
afternoon love scene:

"*Not yet.*"

THE VERNACULOUS OFF-JOURNEY OF

She/He visits it with
his/her
bushel of peevish glass dome quasi-
monolith baby
becomes
ingredient dancing for walk-stop

                      none bother
to sing till some
salient less-so unsung

& barely
collects us a perch in the wise tree
a scraggled a song
sophist
blanket a peace
a xylophone jam in the pause

                      encyclopaedic
:for touching you english for
teasing you greek
that toothsome calisthenic not-speaking-at
                      -all speak
in speeches & call us "a sleep at the station"
to mate-n-obsequious
moments
of de-lish
with the surplice this should shish us (our
orbs
should go leak-ish)

PAPA NOVEMBER

The virgins guard
the emergency glass. Opal
is dying
in her basement house. The numbers station
croons to the spies: *papa november,*
papa november.

Opal: *"alea*
iacta est." The fate
of the empire rests on this. Gardenia,
Delphinium, Gentian, Mum
save their hula
for some
hangers-on.

LOVE CHANT
—for the boys

O well
is wet & never
enough, I stupor for water, you sail
snapwith,
with epi-seeds, across
the lot,
you languisher, you cavalcade, your Novocain, you
nearly are
a traffic jam (to traff
me with), a sprite in dirt, with hands
all forth, a
ring-a-ling & rational, parabolae, a
fluxing
Earth, a feeling up, our
flotsam, alt

•••

kind of tamp & holy
tray
of ash to fell
my cigarette, my scree, my
atlas, high & green—*let's max these tongues*
to firebrand—the devil's
purse, our pessical
of acrid light, our versicle of valiance &
what the way
your skin says mine askance the surf & plasters us
with dovetails born
in desiccants, dissolves them then, dissolves
us thus, *you shoot*
my name
in scattergram

···

& spangled pulse, a sorting of
the salt
of us, let's stew in thrill, let's
torque
in brusk, let's live on *an isthmus of forcible buzz*, in a racket
of clouds, & I'll call you *glitz* & you'll
call me *syringe &*
gunpowder mouth—we're finished up—no we never are, not
ratcheted, but spooling
slow, a hailing hand, a cirrus hand, dry
ice
hello, the sky below, the apertures
slower—so elegant how—&
lowing, never wake us
now

···

morning's throat & navel
play
my flatterman, my strapless cop, my
star to string
the wires up, for peck-to-peck-cum-
appliqué-cum-
exposé-cum-grapefruit tongue & never always dummy
lips, good judge,
injunct,
stay this bouquet, this plea for this, this exigence: *now*
bring us grain to get
us current, break us plenty, make

us gently,
grant us currency, honey, currants, break
with the egg tooth, make
us literally

•••

a sacrosanct,
all sunny sight & sanguine cup, a
splay of fuss &
let us last a future cast—a color cast—another
bite of fructose/glu-
cose
forfeiture to either or utility: we interface
our paler arms, our paler arms
of chromium, our chrome arms of gymnasium, our
coolings cased
in platinum—
                    your denoted truck—

my aptly damnèd plume—

& our axioms of moonstrike & mimetic plumb

CHERRIES

We wanted it far more finger to nose; low pile
on knee-high seats, haywired. We wanted it shamrock,

erotic wind. Bright city: *we're doing it.* Lightning:
come in. We wanted it come to rest on the craps table,

so we would feel so very money storm then.
Better than tens. Whirling lights, then.

We wanted it get down to steer & crustacean,
a triple-cash up to the oompah they were & galleons.

We wanted it so exponential in the gold award castle.
Pluto, oh petunia, can you see we wanted it so extra mega

that we swallowed those lucky & all their ladies, their
trucking & weekend. We were feeler, hoof

& fruit multiplier. We wanted it so sizzling seven,
we fell into a doghouse for king watermelon. For you,

a doghouse, for balloon bars. We did it so diamond deluxe,
we wanted it more pretend, so we did it on Santa's

jackpot bed & felt so very more big pulsar then—

I WOULDN'T CALL IT
'JE NE SAIS QUOI,' EXACTLY

I would, perhaps, call it wretchedness—or emesis. Emesis with gummy worm, partially digested, and an orthodoxy to end all orthodox thoughts: all revolutionary turns. I would call it vomit, in my weaker moments—"bracelet," in my stronger moments—as then, I could take a sharp mouth around the wrist. As in: *the city is pleased to announce that our complete set of allegories has arrived.* The city is pleased, yes.

•••

What The Charms Mean: *I Felt A Face in My Honey Pot, Won a Juicer at the Jr. High, Watched Randy Feel Becky Up, And Then The South Realigned, Becky Turned To God, Becky Has Lymphoma & A Panda Diary, I Am Not Becky, I Saw a UFO—SCARED THE SHIT OUT OF ME, And Once They Said Your Cervix Is Gone I Got Half Stuck In A Tree, An Alien Dressed As A Rabbit Pulled Me Out (Or Tried To), Becky Took Off With A NASCAR Dad (Or Was That Me?), I've Always Thought NASCAR Dads Took Too Long To Squeeze (Now That's A Thing Of The Past), and My Immune System Has Turned On Itself At A Jr. High Dance.*

•••

It is a snafu in my semantic field. It is the arrival of PANAMA CANAL in my semantic field. Before PANAMA CANAL everything came semi-unified from a grapefruit-scented Bohemian in Café Boheme, eating prager schnitzel and avoiding the May Day Parade. PANAMA CANAL just conjures the possibilities of sweat. And sweaty men. And non-reciprocal sex—as in *she turned back the covers and he'd left a single chocolate coin, and on her deathbed, she clutched a single chocolate coin!* Let us not go down that road, again. Let us not do that: there is a pyramid with a floating eye, look. Let us not do that: they are burying small fishes with the corn—*you should know.* Let us turn our attention to the 35-hour work week.

•••

I am sort of allergic—meaning that, well, I'm that besieged. The ivory trade,
Mother Nature, polyglots—all of it. Lochrians jump in the midsection, but I have
turned the shutters down on that hatchery. I am so tired of being right. I am so
tired of predictions. I will be more tired, still, as a spurned integer, a liar. I was once
formidable—I dug mines, lay naked in the mines. The canary shone his light on
me: *yellow thing*, he said—and I couldn't die, and he loved me, like a FIRESIDE
CHAT, for years, and he drank—

THE CORPOREAL OTHER

That one who scribbled a spiral on a chalkboard
& said, "Here is your pinky, here's when I leave."

That one's the hole in the sugarsphere.
Where do they sell those gritty wings? Lawn darts

abstract the lawn. Mother says: "Tell everyone
you love them before they're gone." A death, like a friend,

is sunny June, when you're Georgia peach.
Two children gather in a circle, clasp a doll &

hope the Lord will appear. Where two or more are
gathered in my name—nothing like the absence

where God had been. Like madmen, later, they swore
at the sky. How do you say *my fridge is full,*

when we once starved? God & I picked out the pears.
"Pears," said one, "want something more."

HOW I EXPLAIN MYSELF TO FORMER, CURRENT & POTENTIAL HUSBANDS

I could not find my mittens.

I was the breath on the phone.

I am Aunt Maggie & cool to the touch.

I was a mailman & pregnant with a post office box,

full of final notices from the inner ear.

I am arching & pregnant with dying postulates.

I will be the ellipsis between one & every other.

I am frigging anachronistic, so said all the nuns.

I will float in the music of liminal sounds.

I lived on spent bullet shells for a number of years.

I'm gold & I rim commemorative plates.

I was highly prized jackfruit & then I was rags.

I conduced.

I can hum to the soundest of postulates.

I will misspend my youth on a calf & macramé.

I made like a mitten & prayed for ellipses.

I was afraid of pencils & wary of shale.

I will get pregnant & smash all the commemorative plates.

I'm ashamed of the ambiguous gender of the mail.

I wash the spent bullet shells & diaper the nuns.

Look.

I lived as a nun in a field of shale.

I will wear down my pencils on misspent postulates.

I live as an arching, highly prized jackfruit.

I was Aunt Maggie for a number of years.

I am bullet shells. I'm a frigging anachronist.

I aligned myself with the inner ear.

I pried your damned prick from my liminal ear.

I am prying your damned prick from my liminal ear.

I will pry your damned prick from my liminal ear.

DRINK TO

"I am carried along like a ship without a steersman,
and in the paths of the air, a light, hovering bird;
chains cannot hold me, keys cannot imprison me,
I look for people like me and join the wretches."
—from "Carmina Burana"

The Prisoners

Please, Angel, spinner of *suave*, delete
your palm from fortune, from reed—
read red as location;
one from which the back wall is gray,
is a pin-up of someday sex.

How confusing. How everything can begin again.

Thursday
was freedom—you remember:
diesel & teriyaki, your flavors, Klonopin backdrop
& up on Aurora John.

Is your box murder? Is it
five o' clock? Is it *Taco Del Mar*?
Mark off every day a moonscape of the Mother,
mark every day as *one*.

The Living

The illusion of possession,
a gray granite collection—something
to give away
on her death bed, or a long, last suggestion:

the only thing important is mascara.
Your weight is your place marker. Your smile
will dictate your elevation,
your frown will decide your
temperature. Most importantly,
place matching towels
at your point of origin.

I don't care how.

All Christians

What you think is a halo is a rusty spoon.
Angel waves a knife
& we think it's Apocalypse.

We no longer recognize thunder.
His spring has come & metastasized.
He sings it like an ambulance siren.

Fellow patrons
of fork & prayer, welcome the lion.

The Faithful Dead

In the space from hand to hand, at Pike Place,
sold & played
by swine donors, morels, the King
was thrown, for pleasure, for flash pictures.
Who knew his future

would be dashed by his flesh?
His slapped-butt, paprika, rosemary, brown sugar
are yours in oil, in apricot ale—
the co-sine of '98 *Domaine de Thalabert.*
He listens at lunch—non-empathetic,
poorly socialized bastard & Happy Easter, Happy Summer.

The Loose Sisters

Write it around the old girl,
write it around her, younger.
Wrap it around another foreign body
in the loosie-goosie bed & operate.

Numbers: pH: 164; Lovers: 30 inches;
Muscles: $832.54; Birds: 17; Oftens: 2,146;
Maybes: 2; Nevers: 2;

Drinks: 15,330; Years: 7 & weighing the glass of water—

The Footpads in the Wood

Here is a path. Here is a scythe, see—
the difference is a bathtub & a razorblade
or Florida.
Make your own impetus
from a belt or hairbrush! Look crisp
on the balcony—topographical, *or else.*

The Errant Brethren

A corner of half of the lower face says
he's given up on love & believes in gin.

How noble to swim
in that pine, so redundant—
he says *smells like pine*, so redundant.

The Dispersed Monks

Taxman swipes at elusive fairy
with a golf club & a drink.

She shovels her driveway at the first hint
of snow. Calenture
has come to impart her secular,
most inherent advice: Take a minute
to string clouds into rhetoric. Poems depend on it.

Take Angel, for instance, & his mother,
Repair, who scalds his hands
through prison bars.

The Seamen

Kneel to the poppy mouths who
rifle your bathroom, who
spit & spilled
themselves on flannel

for bent limbs & grasp, & when lonely,
suckle your image like a spring-filled balloon.

You know, by now, girls
are filthy tornadoes & street lamps
reflecting from tanned, mirrored shoulders.
Hold dirty girls by blue light,
be Jared be Todd.

We're just as you imagine—
we're Port-filled vaginas.

The Squabblers

How bumble. How be. So gorgeous & I
have pain in the quadrants,
we break.

Right, taillight kakistocracy, a filmy,
under-worn walk: feet over mountain,
shut aorta, mouth
blocked. You call to the god of birds;
we twitter. We are a blind elbow

& the floor bleeds back, when half my vision.

The Penitent

Hung in the doorway of a smokestack town
is the breath of another son,

relieved.
Mother divined this
from the pickle tray
with help from wrists & surround sound.

See how they lie, pointed in the same direction?

If you swipe,
they move like webworms.

The Wayfarers

Guitar man. That's how I say *long lost man*,
car-door framed. Ganymede, present
in the trailer court driveway.

Ah, swift contrecoup & weed
in the crack
of the union by-laws, union hat.

Angel,
you cupped my breast in July
& you knew we were no good, stuck hard
like dirty gills
& uncombed fins, for years

SKY-LIT HI

Digitally re-mastered from the pluribus tongue,
As clack through the dance hall as all-fall-down better,
Hip bones horde language, barometric or better,
The charge for admission: lip, Tom Collins or tongue.

A girl's just as *frankly* as her maximum hello,
The more thou the than-holy, the more proper the sin,
The more plum the protest, the more *cilia* the sin,
A treble in the palate. Pull taut this hello.

Claim virulence, back-bend & bring down the moon,
A murder of shibboleths, spruce at my thighs,
Soon-to-be-exposed-on-your-rug-or-whatever thighs,
Call me plover, call me petulant, then smile & then moon.

TRAGEDY

—after a painting by David Salle

To continue amongst explosion & couch.
To lay lemons on the floor, to dilly, to mightily

speak of wrists, of slits & birds in the slats. Say, *that
pendulum bird again,* out loud. Do you always mean

such devilish jumps? Is the devil so heavy on that
lissome back? One tries to be a much meatier species, but

sun summers those who sunflower themselves. A premonition
prepares the presupposed: the house numbers will

leave & where will you live? Who'll connect your wild tones?
The sounds, the proficiencies you eye & stroke. Forgive

the eggs despite their shells: from Farmer Bandy's hand,
on the stoop. Chickens that give them are scratches & soup;

you find their heads listening long after. Because you pity
some wings in the porch lamp's glow, things bred cataclysmic,

over & over, like the resonance we fake, like
curved letters & noises; because you pity some legs

in the porch lamp's glow, you hug hard a maxim:
love, so supreme, you shall never love anything

III.

DECREE

Last stab to leave
                    the grandstand &
either a sleeper or a shiny one
gem-encrusted
unfathomed found later
was deemed upon a put upon
slanted man dahlias vendetta & gather
in the blood-soaked pleased
                              to introduce
unchained & the Orange Queen's
gotten loose & horribly
maimed—

TEASER

Labor for coin-fed
lover a tumor
will pull at the heartstrings & sinew
                                          bring tears
sweet hold the prime mover for one long & fair
hapless demise
on the hovel door
you come over bring your scalpel over
nose past the pit kiss the piglet & flee
to the doctor half-dressed in Daphne's
                                          blush
& half-obscured by the leaves breast pink
curtain *oh twinkles you have a thing*
in the ribcage with us
                                  you won't believe

PERSONAL

Crystal's a frosh
        & the crater snug
crystal half-lungs longs for the touch of
a new one knitting into a shallow
breather & yoga & walks on the beach
& hang-ups on your every volcano
ergo for a good time simple
pre-formed cenolithic leg
loves beefalo
wollemi sticks
if you like ferns & fading gills
& neo-kissing
        crystal-fish

NOTICE

Ash limb askew
                    out the orange chiffon
silver deposit in the uterine stretch
& built that house *built every inch*
what's his is his to his
                              transgression
is mine is a gingham field dressed know this
you don't step on look at put one toe on—
it's called a law
because it makes
us one devised civilized fenced
acre on shady you nothing no tantra
no Kleenex flowers
                    no *champ selliezees*

RITE

Will re-visit

      he approximate

remains this honorable estate

an heirloom peach blossom

                  comforter &

reconciliatory

      enjoinder so

slid a bit in her

however shrill

& kept her awake in sickness *I know*

pronounced the protector

of ecumenical bed

Mr. & miniature may & the grave

TOAST

May you finger the lord
                first know each star
the hue of its cradle may you know genitalia
its logos laid down on the porch & cried
hid in a margin
may you find it assign
to each one's ejecta as each one moves
so certain the megalopolis
                      will hold
your schema my schema
will work may we glue
may we get things finite may I make you
gross esoteric clandestine delete
till I say you're small & we'll eat
                      from small plates

WARNING

Spend up a crisp twenty-minute still
to deem the language
of economy is
a chaser you paid in
            ice & mint
aside the sand & the in & out of
whiskey & paltry you are to me
a tiny purse of platitudes
unsaid it barely means a whit
who argued *e pluribus I am so*
alone I crooned to the coin heads heaved
& headed south my love was born
with a silver spoon he has
                no mouth

VOW

Gelastic you-boy
        shackled leg
I'll knapple you duple a furtive of no one's
fenced in my crossed-heart
& hope to play
chalaza-chaser by eve by mourn
I'll kiss your place in their shaving mirrors
all of my ardor my
           triplicate anglers
wrangling for bronchio-meso-*my little*
rabbit has bought me his tail
              end
of the junket hey jeff jeremiah wade aidan

CONFESSION

Make wind the arbiter

                        my own two hands
full sine forsaken I've long diseased
from icons satellites light born breaker
breaker a-one two digging for gems
to catch just one white sprite on the line
one in an elevator
one in pearls
as much like empathy or stricken from
sympathy sleep off the atmosphere
I did them all impulse & moisture

                                    there
in the dank-soft earth or if they were
a collection of say it

                    sorryworms

WARRANTY

Should it basically
        & go multi-celled
do not dismiss it as lightly as some
roundtable on/off tantamount mean
exhibits a quaver
cannot be fed
handle Baby Hospitable Clean
good on your pulley your inclined
                        plane
unhook said motto from powdered head
flexures & sigmoids
on the blankie or
paints
        the sun lounge in pre-schoolers' blood

MORAL

What is that redolent thing

     the green

spear of an eye
root of the gall
the details are intricate *shot up a mall*
if the body looses us lickety trees
on dandified trees &

    when the tongue

teases some triune what does it do
for the long over-arching long arm of the long
to a bright assertion the bud responds
to a vis-à-vis
or is it a *vaz*
or searching the cream on each

      other's nose

TRACT

& yea though I waltz
                    tasered & dowsed
through humerus mazes of quasars & brim-
stone sterna between thyself & thy
providence gave us
solar roses
of red-skinned urchins who lurk in the ions
of earthlings whoever
                    so loved the world
in pistils & stun-gunned the clean of hark
shall hark ever-lasting & sore
                              the pinks
shall inherit a petiole-tarsal garden

IV.

ONTOGRAPHY

Habromania (Birth)

Born acute,
fragment of blame, of jilted age & lipstick
case—strung rind
to rind &
temple to temple & true to name, carved
eyes in it &
wore its poorish cranium.

Skip the top note so
I increase, or
skip the big bang for another buffet.

My love shall fetter,
underwater. My sucklings will carry
the scepter, across.

Abscission (Girlhood)

& went unto
Peace Prince Strawberry Pie: *became*
a restive & egregious one, put salt
in the pudding, cut
the light, refused his ganglia, prepared
for home.
"I have yet to lay
my tongue to the silt. I will never risk a honeymoon—"

With a pocket of eggs, the spoils. The sea,
by which I scramble, rigs
this clean.

Lickerish (Education)

Mitochondria
told me another one. He has
taken the placemat & left the mince (which was my
whole plan to get right, again).
Went on about latitude
& wind
from the south. Had *a merriment* with coconut, one without
coconut milk (he, desperate, promised
a moon slice & never did)

& was rude, (went out
for my good
heart) beside the pyramid, before
the polis. So
he "lay in a manger." *High-born oligarch—*

Teleonomy (Stock)

The pre-sun
echoes the dire question. A backhoe
uncovered
the body, Saturn:

*"In a pocket, silly, it was there
all the time—"*

—made necklaces
for me to wear, of
turquoise apostrophe, actuary's

crumb. Go back
to the matter from which
you came.

Callisteia (Love)

I'll see
your ovary & a tumult
of weeks—"Tell me, Brimstone: is the body
meek
with talons &—*what
anatomy for flame!*"

Leviathan gets me dizzy—*so there*
(& unhooks
the second head, green &
pale)

"... *& lo, the foragers stopped
the hunt
for ions enamored, the theory
of lift
& jubilarians, in their
fantasies, kept
the vanilla in (sin) with the penicillin...*"

Malmsy (The Disillusionment)

Scorched earth: a tarsal
melting, here. What's behind

that shade could turn the elements & grow—
Lemon, please. Lemon, yes. My name
is Mandy-Mind-the-Lace.

(My past looms like
a mothership
& as the mothers said: to be un-held &
pigeonholed.) Bow
& string.
Dissonant, despondent. Tuesday morning.

Reliquiae (Resolve)

Gondola
left me, lanugo gone, in a holding
pattern & after-effect:

MY SCAFFOLD WHERE MY LADDER WAS

And then, the rain
lets up & I'm
at once the brightest sycophant,
three times
around the lesser ring:
my yellows, curios, pinks & after—
the transfer of k/cals
& the whole bleak continent does
mingle
with the bleeders, hos, toxins,
a small while.

A SUCCESSION OF BLACKSHIRTS

Console generale, I live
in a poster. *Console,* where a rust sun comes up
in the corner. *Primo seniore,* the foxes
are filing. *Seniore,* a fresh
doxological head.

Centurione, make new
the feet. *Capo manipolo,*
& a whirlwind in bed. *Sottocapo manipolo,*
the year minus is. *Aspirante*
Sottocapo manipolo, so we are.

Primo Aiutante, all elbows
& knees. *Aiutante capo,* you'll wear
a dress of non-. *Aiutante,* lain doggo
& cooed in a line. *Primo*
capo squadra, bonhomie.

Capo squadra, roots to
undo. *Vicecapo squadra,* the mouth
of the matron. *Camicia nera scelta,* so vitamins.
Camicia nera, & the true-
stay untrue.

TRINITY W/CITRUS

When the girl was just a viscous plane,
the ghost was only
being born.
The egg presents to the focus group:
racecar for ghost, skin for girl.
She pours a foundation
to honor concrete. The ghost makes a ceiling
for her viscous skin. She's pink
& the focus group's read her whole dossier:
peccatophobic,
desperate to pave.
The egg leaves decisions dead, in the dirt.
The ghost denounces
a dram of limes,
who rejected their locules.
We must not hatch here.

What scared her shoulder
down to its wheel? Why are we
precious & twining like mayflies?
The egg & the girl
have improvised pains. The ghost
by the lime grove
rejected the limes.
Racecar meant exhilaration; skin, tear within,
meant *consult the focus group*
as soon as you can.
Even pecks later & bushels past.
Even after the hailstorm stops.

The racecar in the ghost
is the viscous girl.

She's pining for asphalt. The egg
is supercool. Light from the lime grove
bathes the green sinner. Light from the sinner
makes the lime grove, just so.

BARN

As I have become irrefutably obsolete, so has the blush peach fallen lusciously into the yard. I recall how I brought the tree home. My young pigtails, aflame. In this one visual image, I hold a million suns on my shoulder. In the Kingdom of Peaches each has his philosophy branded on the inside of a pelt. At night, they quietly read. I say everyone has a hidden name and today we are very, very close to hearing them.

•••

Let us not be proud for the fine print, but be proud for pride. It, too, engenders a chemical reaction and clean rooms. Sparkling clean rooms that let the flora see a tear for their own exacerbations. A moss catching its reflection in a terrine, having a moment of epiphany—a good clear admiration for the moon. This impulse carries all other impulses inside it. And for a moment I want to marry the moss. And you think it's beautiful and you'll cry at our wedding. I'm wearing a white dress, the sea is churning the background and I'm marrying a small heap of moss in front of our families and friends. The sky cleared up for us at this moment. And I am so genuinely happy that I've made this choice. I feel lucky and blessed and ready to begin my life as a wife.

•••

The discarded stockings lay on the floor like time. The bend of me makes a beautiful doorway for your mother's death. This is all the ancient I can locate amongst the reference material. Still, I sit sipping on a straw, staring at myself staring at melting fungi. I saw you there—when the room disappeared. The low note of laughter turned you into my house. I was rabid with joy—please turn into a bird again. That kind of transformation allows me to remember.

•••

At this distance, the echo is perfect. Twin sentiments ring out over the heaps of wheat. Why must you why must you go on putting your corpuscles go on putting

your corpuscles outwards toward me and I outwards toward me and I am the love
that you imagined am the love that you imagined only with more love than you
only with more love than you imagined which made me imagined which made me
weak and scared made me weak and scared

MY ONE PANELED WALL

There are one trillion ways to say *my one*
paneled wall. Such as, *any necklace is*

too tight, the air has been punched out
of breakfast, the scenario involves many

ceremonies of lypo & lipids, or the eyes have
it. Beauty is the only recourse, she says & pencils

& forks insist they're liked best lined up
& facing northward. At the moment

of your death, she says, you must have
courtesy samples of lipsticks & eye shadows

to divvy amongst your hungry nieces. Heat
sticks to smile & ass, indivisible. Fire

in the cheeks sticks, stumbling over his till. The
tremor of fruit, faintly. The fork whispers:

northward. A word for "fucking miracle."

HAND, FLOOR, GALAXY

& plot means plumb
to particular women, who've little pea & little play.
My rigs are stalling
on bitumen, & figs are great & figs are gay.
I'm set to weeping on light/predicate/dark—cabbage punching,
until I can't stop: *the revolution*
will not be televised, lover
& the verboten camels,
the cancer happy, promised we'd sleep
a more ontological supper.

In present tense, the puppet takes
a puppet
to task in the ticklish sense.
They bump tables of contents,
set their glossaries afloat on the octagonal memories
of indefensible men
& their reviled quasi-qi clock kinetics, (she bore him
a ham submarine in the sink)
& the breaded & hard-fried moon, marooned
in the clunk

of colliding puppet stink,
is the theory of oratory sell-by date,
tripping to cast
the swine before Pearl & The Polyester 8.

You can't handle the truth
if it's longer than daytime, from hilt to cap,
on the merry-go-round of the plumbers, all smitten
in logotherapy pant
& juvies
have their knees touching. Puberty works.

If I go out *bushido*,
I'm technological rat.
If my rhyme was a drug, I'd sell it by the gram,
& snort myself up, as the planets
plan it.

(In the snow globe of torpor, senators, flamingoes
down bottles
of hound's blood & Red No. 40,
as it is the cure
for the tender maladies.
As it is the best cure for the most tender
melodies.)

SMALL THINGS INDUSTRIES

I thought it looked beautiful over there. Commercial zoning or death. Why, you ask, do people display their plates? All I can think of is a womb filled with plates. A raggedy Anne and raggedy Andy, sewn to blessedness: teens' lips, locked. A science looms in our sunrises, tinted orange-red.

•••

We have a policy about your policy. The first is that you can leave if you take your policy with you. If you insist on continuing, we'll create a filter for you. Placentas will burn everywhere around you, baguette crust will crack and be thrust in olive oil, people will pale in mid-conversation and you will have none of it. If you're good, I'll add "Her Most Alienating Cunt," and the cat's tongue will push through a thin membrane. You can and will accuse her, but you will never see her face.

•••

The politics have been handled. The hairless baby rats oblige. It is quiet in this conservatory, at last. Denouement absorbs all the "otherwise" noise. I wait for nothing to happen. For artlessness to reach its apex, I must mean what I say. I must show you a bird in black and white, and tell you what's inside of it: critique and desire. *And it became more and more boring as I told it.* I studied the edge of your window—your one eye on the junipers. The candy girls found your brilliance inside them. I finally did shoot myself. And I didn't mean to tell it any more than you did.

•••

We were not meant to fly. Or I was not meant to wear spring green, my palms sweaty. Even now—that turn—even now, as she billows the sheets in the laundries, even now as we press our advances out over the courtyards, even now as the chervil burns in the credenza...

CHA-CHA-CHA

One small rumor
is running wild: They're building a factory
out of your backstory & solving
the matrix
where the wings attach, for six sextants of love
in the sloeberry sloughs.

You, like wish. You,
like every bird footprint
in bricks. We like
aggrandized, elite exercise. Punch-knuckle
puzzle, punch-knuckle
puzzle:

"This statement is a left-brained, beatified lie."

When the sun
began spitting at its homophone,
the Fair Scone War had raged
one thousand springs.
Many fools proofed the primary script:
You got in a cattle car, they removed your rings, pitched
your teeth
to the priests: covet & cope. Spines snapped—
the new nouns were too heavy:
You're no Jack Kennedy, no calling plan, no
ruby—

Strumpet, you're the trumpet's tuba envy.

•••

Do us a favor:
If propellers
don't prop the profligate, or even
good pies get spurned,
then buy a pistol
& buy a dress. Stuck, the dress.
Sore, a purse.
Eyes on the lawn jockey.

Pox

on the universe.

Rude shelter of rouge
(Rages one jillion autumns…)
Makes you sexy
& a trigger.
Jiggle for knee jerk. Sleep
for England.

V.

TU QUOQUE

Say
your baby is mine & your
baby is
a butterfly & caught
himself
a butterfly. Butterfly
knows
what your baby keeps, deep
in the ear
of its labyrinth, a butterfly
knows
where the body is your baby colored
impulse red
& hammer blue & hammer blue. Say
my baby butterfly
is you
& makes my dick a tree-shaped cloud. Say
but, my baby's
hands
are clean & butterfly *sliced from groin to chest*
& say my butterfly
never was
& your baby's a freckle, found
in the leaves.

TO NOT BE PERPLEXED
ABOUT THE GIVENS

It comes
in handy on a cheap date co-
belligerent
& foot full of splinters

your wingèd

bent over an egg sack
in thin channel tele-
ology of the
tell-all:

hot gar
hot body

THE FLOWERS OF KUNGSHALLEN

A logic problem for girls & boys

The red
begonias must be planted
adjacent to
the pink petunias. The pink petunias
must
be planted where she
relaxes & starts to like it. She cannot like it
in the frontal lobe, the atria, the
pinky toe. The white begonias must
be planted where she relaxes & starts

to fold. She cannot like it on hot formica, not
stringendo, not
on retainer, so
the pink snapdragons must be planted
where she relaxes & starts to falter. She likes it so
that a tongue is a pulley, a pulley's
a screw & a screw
is a lever. The red
snapdragons must be pressing
in concert
with the vague abstention. The appended action
precedes

the motion. Bull foot, fulcrum, per-
mutation. The rash fruition must be loosed
where she relaxes
& starts
to juice. She cannot like it in the lemon
forest, the second chorus, the leaf
unmooring. She must be planted in the patch
occurring where she

relaxes
& starts to churning. The pink begonias'
pat intangibles: servant, stem-wound,
supine, triggered. The yellow snapdragons must
be practiced
where you're too trickle & she's
beleaguered. Full of states she's hastened, lessened
pressure-washed
porch &
cutlets, peaches. The peach-cum-plaintiff must
be plated
where she's a party & she's
a party.

SITTING THE BATOLOGIST
—after a signature

So-staved sating slight
or hand
side-wound in this seem-stressed
primus paeon's
had her child & thinks
it's to pray
for some
clear derelict from dawn or dearth

O
sloth
to escape that
soonscape fluorescent
hell
& the brambles & the
bees-all of my lovers
forked over what one prosed path of slither
fled
me to an utter bed   the other to mother

gives a possible plural
pleasant
non-trinkety etude &
neurasthenic

so what you sew don't know oh
to stay it

sorta
so assail
some
scrap to the ether:

& I don't know how to stitch it, either):

        what steers
        planchette from placenta
        to suture

        to *post aut propter*   & ergo "to suit her"

ALPHABUG

We have momentarily
lost our joy. Our very protons
are plotting against us, as we lie on the rug,
talking of letters. I know "C"
as abulia blue, to you,
she's red—you keep telling me. We know
of ourselves that which is lesser, though
we spell out the greater. Alphabug,
to thine own appendages
be dictator, be true.
Thine own punctilio, increase.

You never blink.

Shall we meet at the entry of milium & milk?
Shall I come as Mother,
repressed & replete? When they find my boy,
face down, in a pool, I'll cry ten times
the pool & maybe
ten times
my drink. Oh, Alphabug,

our diseases
are approaching & we
might never bloom. We may never
go forth & plant a psychic kiss
in an irreducible room,
or wear our green cheeks
out. We pray: Oh coathanger, clothespin,
plate—our outlooks,
our pull cords
are the cruces of these days &

derelicts we are, but more than the sum
of some simple eyes &
prolegs &

then, we say it again. *Amen. Amen.* Should we find

the perfect pines for our caskets
& mark them, plainly,
with my "O"s & your "X"s, tomorrow,
we'll lolly,
fictitious & vapors. Today,

we say: *no masses, no metastasis.*

VIRTUE, CONTINENCE, INCONTINENCE, VICE

Pretty kitty embolus
curlers & pins
up our conscience tries
like a tick
to give back the cookie jar & the lute
is the sound
our heart made *our veins*
didn't want too-

guilty Plato did her hair up in miss-
no-good outcome the
clot
could dissolve
& we'll skip down the staircase & just then it was
ascending on tiny
yellow legs
in knee-socks white boots feline
the hand
that pets itself all-platelet
senses

arrest in the all-night eyes on the body's
hackles
declines *Aristotle's egregious*
dress-up
for bed is where we
purr:

sorry & not finished taking you
                    back

then Plato's collar was a way of life
that
pulsed like
we were prisoners of *look*:

      Aristotle
      bounced down the steps *a lark*
      & stepped on it
      & tried
      to stand it back up

THE STAR CHILDREN

Dear Jupiter,

if not
this moon
that keeps the guts
from spilling out, it has to be
your *other* moon that
holds in the hidden baby.

We sunned,
southside, a muscle wall. Polaris
put his hands on me. *I love you. I love*
what you've given me: poor
skin turgor, sunken
eye.

Hope this holiday, you find
an "inner peace,"

        Polaris & Crystal,
        Callisto, Cholera, Jejunum & Ileum,
        Azimuth & False
        Dilemma.

THE FALLACY OF MISLEADING VIVIDNESS

Could not close the consciousness gap. Could not turn bus driver from cherry to flame to inamorato to flame. I could not find the key to his golden hair, neither his lyre, and when I talked he pretended to be asleep. That is, when I talked I pretended to be asleep. I could not make him pleasure himself nor you nor me nor anyone.

•••

I saw it in the hallway, I saw it in the parlor. It was on the faces of the cows. I saw it in "Music Box Dancer," I saw it in an epilepsy. It was writhing on my dentist's wet arm, it lurked in the bottom of the umbrella stand. It was in an old purse and then on an old tray. In the night garden, it beckoned me. In bed, it showed its fangs. In a backflash, I was tuned in. And I succumbed and I succumbed and I succumbed.

•••

Are you sure you don't remember that day.

•••

When it snows, they shut the city down. Chihuahuas contemplate cuneiform: three strangled owls. "*Bitch, Bitch, Bitch,*" whispers one small dog. Children slide down hills.

The poem "Tragedy" first appeared in *The Canary*. The poem "Cherries" first appeared in *Interim*. The poems "Love Chant," and "Executive Branch" first appeared in *Denver Quarterly*. The poems "Decree," "Teaser," "Notice," "Toast," and "Warranty" first appeared in *Action, Yes*. The poems "Warning" and "Tract" first appeared in *Cranky*. The poems "A Succession of Blackshirts" and "Eileen" appeared in *The Bedazzler* and *The Hat*. The poem "Tu Quoque" first appeared in *VERSE*. The poems "Virtue, Continence, Incontinence, Vice," "Vow," "Confession," "Automated Floorness/Ceilingness Questionnaire," "Alphabug," "Ontography," and "The Flowers of Kungshallen" first appeared in *The Bedazzler*. The poem "Rite" first appeared in *The Tiny*. The poems "That Which We Pull From Air Has Always Been, " "Drink To," and "Papa November" first appeared in *No-Tell Motel*. The poem "The Corporeal Other" first appeared in *Open City*. The poem "My One Paneled Wall" first appeared in *Conduit*. The poem "Warning" is dedicated to Peter Stuhlmann.

The author would like to thank Nico Vassilakis, her family and friends, Dara Wier, Slope Editions, D.A. Powell, G.C. Waldrep, James Galvin, The Iowa Writers' Workshop, Cosa Nostra Editions, Adam Grano and Caroline Cabrera.